W9-AFS-649

First Facts®

Feasts in Ancient Times

the BIG PICTURE

CAPSTONE PRESS
a capstone imprint

Anna Claybourne

First Facts is published by Capstone Press, a Capstone imprint,
151 Good Counsel Drive, P.O. Box 669, Mankato, Minnesota 56002.
www.capstonepub.com

First published in 2010 by A&C Black Publishers Limited, 36 Soho Square, London W1D 3QY
www.acblack.com
Copyright © A&C Black Ltd. 2010

Produced for A&C Black by Calcium. www.calciumcreative.co.uk

042010
005769ACS11

Library of Congress Cataloging-in-Publication Data
Claybourne, Anna.
  Feasts in ancient times / by Anna Claybourne.
    p. cm. — (First facts, the big picture)
  Includes index.
  ISBN 978-1-4296-5541-5 (library binding) — ISBN 978-1-4296-5542-2 (pbk.)
  1. Food habits—History—Miscellanea—Juvenile literature. 2. Fasts
and feasts—History—Miscellanea—Juvenile literature. 3. Dinners and
dining—History—Miscellanea—Juvenile literature. I. Title. II. Series.

GT2850.C55 2011
394.1'209—dc22   2010024404

Every effort has been made to trace copyright holders and to obtain their permission for use of copyright material.
This book is produced using paper that is made from wood grown in managed, sustainable forests. It is natural,
renewable and recyclable. The logging and manufacturing processes conform to the environmental regulations
of the country of origin.

Acknowledgements

The publishers would like to thank the following for their kind permission to reproduce their photographs:

Cover: Wikimedia Commons (front), Shutterstock: Michael Ledray (back). **Pages:** Corbis: Francis G. Mayer
18; Istockphoto: Horst Klinker 14; Photolibrary: Fotosearch 12; Shutterstock: Almagami 16-17, Anky 9, Andrey
Armyagov 20, Brian Chase 2-3, 6-7, Cobalt88 14-15, Digital Studio 4-5, Ioana Drutu 12-13, Melinda Fawver 15,
Gordon Galbraith 10-11, Eric Isselée 17, Javarman 22-23, Margrit Kropp 3, Michael Ledray 6, Martina I Meyer
20-21, Mountainpix 8-9, Andrei Nekrassov 24, Objectsforall 10, Omkar A V 18-19, Seregam 4, Kachalkina
Veronika 16, Dvoretskiy Igor Vladimirovich 13; Wikimedia Commons: 1, 5, 11.

Contents

Feast!

In ancient times, most food was pretty boring. People ate bread, rice, or porridge—for every meal.

Living it up

In the castles or palaces of Europe, it was a different story. Huge **feasts** were held, with meat, giant cakes, and lots more.

Boring!

Look at me!

A big castle feast wasn't just about having a good meal. Rich people had feasts to show off to their friends or **rulers**.

Servants waited on rich people at castle feasts.

5

At the Castle

Some kings or lords threw parties in their castles and made sure the guests ate amazing food.

Roast dolphin

Castle cooks roasted birds, such as swans and herons. They even served dolphin!

Peacock was often on the menu at feasts.

Spicy and pricey

People ate sauces made with **spices** and fruits. These came from faraway places, so they cost a lot of money.

Peacock pie

Roman Party

The ancient Romans loved parties. Rich people had parties with huge feasts in their houses.

Showing off

Romans served up different-sized birds—stuffed inside each other. They liked to eat food that was hard to find, such as birds' tongues.

Tall order

I feel sick!

The Romans loved to stuff themselves full of food. Sometimes they were sick because they had eaten too much. Disgusting!

Very rich Romans sometimes ate giraffes.

Hot Dogs

Montezuma was a great Aztec leader in Mexico. He had an amazing palace. He also loved eating!

Cooked Aztec

Montezuma ate roast turkey and dogs. Some people say the Aztecs even ate each other sometimes!

The Aztecs loved roasted snake.

Ssssssss

Cocoa crazy

The Aztecs made the first chocolate drink from **cocoa beans**. No sugar was added, so it didn't taste sweet like the chocolate we drink today.

Chinese Feast

A long time ago, an **explorer** called Marco Polo went to China. He stayed with a great leader, Kublai Khan.

Great dining room

Khan had an amazing palace. His dining hall was made of silver and gold. It was so big that thousands of people could eat there.

Kublai Khan served camel milk at his parties.

Ice cream too

In China, Marco tasted ice cream and **noodles** for the first time. He also drank horse and camel milk served in golden cups.

Milkshake?

13

Sun King

Louis XIV was a king of France. He was such a great king that he was called the Sun King.

Eat, eat, eat

Louis held amazing feasts. People ate five **courses**, and each course had 50 different dishes.

Louis had a sweet tooth and loved to eat cakes.

To die for

Louis' cooks took their job very seriously. One even killed himself because the fish he had ordered to cook for the king was not delivered!

Fishy business

Viking Feast

The Vikings were scary fighters who attacked other lands. But they also loved to cook and had big feasts.

Party time

Vikings had a big feast during the **harvest** each year. They held it in a huge village house called a longhouse.

The Vikings loved parties – and fighting!

Chop, chop!

The Vikings ate with a knife. They used it to chop up their food, then stab and grab it. They ate lots of fish, **seal**, and meat such as **boar**.

Never boaring!

Spice Kings

Great kings ruled India a long time ago. They were called Mughals, and they loved to eat spicy food.

Get stuffed!

One Mughal king's favorite food was an egg stuffed inside a small bird, stuffed inside a chicken, stuffed inside a goat, stuffed inside a camel. Phew!

Mughal palaces were filled with wonderful paintings.

Hot, hot, hot

Perfect palace

The Mughals built amazing palaces which they decorated with painted wall tiles, rugs, and beautiful paintings.

Babylon

A long time ago, people lived in a place called Babylon. They had wonderful feasts.

Left behind

We know what the people in Babylon ate because they left their recipes behind.

Boinggg!

Hopping snack

Don't miss the roasted grasshoppers! The Babylonians loved this crispy, crunchy insect. It was a favorite snack.

The Babylonians loved a crunchy grasshopper!

Glossary

Aztec people who lived in South America a long time ago

boar piglike animal with sharp tusks

cocoa beans beans that are made into chocolate

courses stages of a meal, such as an appetizer, main course, and a dessert

explorer person who travels to other places to find out what they are like

feasts great parties where people eat lots of food

guests people who are invited to a party

harvest time when crops are ready to be picked

noodles a long, stringy food a little like spaghetti

rulers people who are in charge

seal animal with flippers that lives in cold places

servants people who worked for rich rulers

spices ingredients that make food taste good

Further Reading

FactHound offers a safe, fun way to find Internet sites related to this book. All of the sites on FactHound have been researched by our staff.

Here's all you do:

Visit www.facthound.com

FactHound will fetch the best sites for you!

Books

They Ate What?! The Weird History of Food by Richard Platt, Two-Can Publishing (2006).

Food and Cooking in Ancient Rome by Clive Gifford, Power Kids Press (2010).

Food and Cooking in Viking Times by Clive Gifford, Power Kids Press (2010).

Index

24